Zurich & Geneva Travel Guide

Attractions, Eating, Drinking, Shopping & Places To Stay

Lisa Brown

Copyright © 2014, Astute Press
All Rights Reserved.

No part of this publication may be reproduced, stored in a retrieval system, or transmitted, in any form or by any means without the prior written permission of the publisher, nor be otherwise circulated in any form of binding or cover other than that in which it is published and without similar condition being imposed on the subsequent purchaser.

If there are any errors or omissions in copyright acknowledgements the publisher will be pleased to insert the appropriate acknowledgement in any subsequent printing of this publication.

Although we have taken all reasonable care in researching this book we make no warranty about the accuracy or completeness of its content and disclaim all liability arising from its use

Table of Contents

Zurich 6
    Culture 8
    Location & Orientation 9
    Climate & When to Visit 10

Sightseeing Highlights 11
    Banhofstrasse 11
    Niederdorfstrasse 13
    Schiffbau Entertainment District 14
    Schipfe, Old Town 16
    Zurich Churches 17
        Grossmünster 18
        Fraumünster 19
        St. Peterskirche 20
    Zurich Museums 21
        Zurich Museum of Art 22
        Swiss National Museum 23
        Museum of Design 24
        Museum Rietberg 26
    Guild Houses 27
        Zunfthaus zur Meisen 27
        Haus zum Rüden, ... 28
    Lindt Chocolate Factory 29
    Zurich Zoo & Masoala Rainforest 30

Recommendations for the Budget Traveller 32
    Places To Stay 32
        Design Hotel Plattenhof 32
        The Guests' House 33
        Hotel Hottingen 33
        Alexander 34
        Hotel Marta 35
    Places To Eat & Drink 36
        Lily's Stomach 36
        Delicato 36
        Kaserne-Shilpost 37
        Volkshaus 38

>   Vulkan 38
> - **Places to Shop** 39
>   - Bahnhofstrasse & Niederdorfstrasse 39
>   - 16 Tons 40
>   - Teddy's Souvenir Shop 41
>   - Bürkliplatz Flea Market 41
>   - Kanzlei Flea Market 42
>   - Speciality Market at Zürich Main Station 42

- **Geneva** 43
    - Culture 45
    - Location & Orientation 46
    - Climate & When to Visit 47
- **Sightseeing Highlights** 48
    - Lake Geneva (Boat Cruises & Swimming) 48
    - St. Peter's Cathedral (Old Town) 50
    - United Nations Building 53
    - Carouge Neighborhood 54
    - Bastions Park 56
    - Place du Molarde 57
    - Paquis (Beach, Baths & Ethnic Eateries) 58
    - Plainpalais Flea Market 60
    - Museum of the Red Cross 61
    - The Saleve (Swiss Alps) 62
- **Recommendations for the Budget Traveller** 64
    - **Places to Stay** 64
        - Hotel Central 65
        - Appart'Hôtel Résidence Dizerens 65
        - Ibis Geneve Central Gare Hotel 66
    - **Places to Eat & Drink** 67
        - Buvette Bains des Paquis 67
        - Le Thé 68
        - Chez Ma Cousine 68
        - Maison Rouge 69
    - **Places to Shop** 70

Zurich

Zürich is Switzerland's largest city and international financial center and has a quaint old town center combined with a delightful riverside. Located on the shore of Lake Zurich it offers a stunning view of the Alps only a short train ride away.

The city is an exciting destination for the outdoors-lover as well as those who like fine dining, nightlife, arts and culture.

You don't have to leave the city to enjoy the pleasures of the countryside. There are a number of outdoor public baths along the river Limmat where you can go for a swim, in addition to many beaches by the lake where you can also rent sailboats. The water in Zurich is so clean that locals use city fountains to refill their water bottles.

Zurich has just as much to offer in the way of urban attractions. Its medieval Old Town is a maze of narrow streets with a plethora of modern clubs and shops. You will also find that many of the picturesque Renaissance guild and town halls house art galleries and cultural institutions. The tree-lined lakeside promenade and the boulevard along the Limmat, popular with both locals and tourists, are always bustling with life, as is the entertainment district along the Niederdorfstrasse.

Repeatedly named as the city with the best quality of life in the world, small wonder Zurich attracts many foreigners; of the nearly 400,000 people who live here, about a third are not Swiss citizens. In the past, the city became a temporary home to artists such as James Joyce, Thomas Mann or Richard Wagner, and it was here that the famous Dada movement began.

Culture

Zurich loves art in all its forms and hosts several annual events highlighting different genres of music and art. The Street Parade, the largest street party in the world, doubles as a techno and dance music festival, and attracts around 1 million participants each year. Those with a taste for more traditional music will fall in love with the Zurich Opera, offering a world class program and housed in an awe-inspiring building that is a rich mix of different architectural styles from neo-Classicism to Rococo.

In 2012, the city organized a street festival of fine art called ART IN THE CITY, devoted to contemporary art from all over the world. Art works were exhibited in the streets throughout the summer (June-September) and were accessible to the public free of charge. The famous art fair Kunst Zurich takes place over three days each November and showcases contemporary visual art from 80 galleries from all over the world. The city also organises more irregular public exhibitions of modern sculptures, with the tongue-in-cheek themes including lions, cows and giant flowerpots.

Don't worry if you're in Zurich on a rainy day - there is just plenty to do here indoors, as well. The Zurich Film Festival has been rising in prominence in recent years; it takes place at the end of September and attracts 60,000 visitors. There are lots of art galleries and museums worth visiting, too. The Zurich Museum of Art holds a vast collection of classic modern art, including works of Picasso, Munch, or Giacometti. Cabaret Voltaire, the birthplace of the Dada movement, offers a varied cultural program that honors the dada tradition, as well as a shop with dada-inspired souvenirs.

Location & Orientation

http://www.stadt-zuerich.ch/vbz/en/index.html

Zurich is located about 30km north of the Alps on the northern end of Lake Zurich. Largely flat, its historic center is spread across the top of a small natural hill called Lidenhof. The banks of the river Limmat have been densely built-up over the years and are an important feature of the city landscape. The Limmat meets another river, the Sihl, close to the Swiss National Museum.

Zurich Airport is a busy international airport that is situated 10km northeast of the city. It is easily reached by train and it takes 10 minutes to reach Zurich Hauptbanhof, the city's main train station. Trains are a popular means of transport as frequent express services connect Zurich with domestic destinations as well as with major cities in the neighbouring countries.

The city transport consists of trams, buses and S-Bahn (overground city trains), all painted blue-and-white. The zone system means ticket prices vary depending on where you want to go, but you will very likely stay within the Zone 110 which covers most of the city proper. A 2nd class day pass for a single zone is CHF8.40 while a single ticket, valid for up to half an hour, costs CHF4.20. You can save money by buying a multiple journey ticket which will give you six single journeys at the cost of CHF22.60.

Climate & When to Visit

http://www.weather-forecast.com/locations/Zurich/forecasts/latest

Zurich has a humid continental climate with four distinct seasons. Summers are very warm, with average high temperatures between 22.5C (72.5F) and 25C (77C). You will likely see some snow if you visit in the winter, when the average temperatures often drop to -3.1C (26.4F).

There is plenty to do in Zurich all year round. Outdoor swimming areas are open May through September. November is a good time to take the mountain train to the top of Uetliberg (15 minutes from the city center, CHF17) which offers a famous panorama of the city. In the winter, you can choose between two open-air ice skating rinks or take a short train ride to the nearest ski resort. The rich cultural program will keep you entertained regardless of the season or weather.

Sightseeing Highlights

Banhofstrasse

Sprüngli, Banhofstrasse 21, 8022 Zurich,
tel. 0041 44 224 47 11
http://business.spruengli.ch/spruengli-filialen.php

Widder Bar, Rennweg 7, 8001 Zurich,
tel. 0041 224 25 26
http://www.widderhotel.ch/widder-bar/index.html?seo=1

You would never guess the humble beginnings of this world famous shopping street: it used to be a swampy area known by the name of Fröschengraben, or "frogs' ditch".

One of the world's most expensive and most famous shopping streets, the posh Banhofstrasse has a string of shiny shop fronts that stretch for almost a mile. Walking down this pedestrian-only zone is a must when you're in Zurich, worth checking out even if you don't feel like buying a necklace from Swarovski or the latest bag from Louis Vuitton.

Start at the main train station and walk along the tree-lined avenue all the way to the lakeshore where you can take a break before going back along the other side. Banhofstrasse is a visual treat in any season: beautifully green in the summer and glimmering with stunning Christmas lights in the winter.

When the window-shopping wears you out, take a break at the oldest chocolate shop in the world, Sprüngli. Founded in 1836, it has had a shop at the same address since 1859. Mouth-watering chocolates are miniature works of art, and if chocolate is not your thing, try their delicious Luxemburgerli, or scrumptious little macarons.

Take a break at Max Bill's Pavilion-Sculpture, a granite Stonehenge-like arts installation doubling as seating space. Escape the crowds by exploring the side streets a little bit. At the end of your day, why not have a drink at the cozy Widder bar on Rennweg Street while listening to some live jazz.

Niederdorfstrasse

Arthouse Alba, Zähringerstrasse 44, 8001 Zurich,
tel. 0041 44 250 55 40
http://www.arthouse.ch/kino/alba

Andorra, Münstergasse 20, 8001 Zurich,
tel. 0041 44 252 65 70
http://www.andorra.ch/index.php

Running parallel to the River Limmat, this cobblestoned narrow street is part of the historic Old Town. Niederdorfstrasse is the up-and-coming entertainment district of Zurich, a pedestrian-only zone always bursting with life, with thousands of people tracing back and forth between innumerable boutiques and restaurants.

A shopaholic's paradise by day, it transforms at night when its many clubs and bars open. In the winter, the Christmas market takes over, offering handmade trinkets and sweets, including traditional Swiss gingerbread.

Niederdorfstrasse was home to the oldest cinema in Zurich and there are still many cinemas operating here today. Most of them favour low-budget productions, although you may see sometimes some mainstream films as well. If it rains, why don't you check out Arthouse Alba, a gem of the 1950s cinema architecture, complete with a stage and a two-tier seating area with balconies. With their rich program including low-budget and Hollywood productions, both old and new, you will surely find something for yourself.

There are lots of bars and pubs to choose from if you feel like winding down a bit. Try Andorra for an enormous selection of Swiss and Belgian beers (around 30 different types are available on tap) and a cocktail menu that lists over 100 different concoctions. And all that served to you while you enjoy some live jazz in a classy and cozy atmosphere.

Take one of the steep alleyways down to the riverfront, or jump on the funicular which will bring you to the university campus. The funicular, operated by vintage cars and painted bright red, first opened in 1889, and today is sometimes called "Student Express" because of its location.

Schiffbau Entertainment District

Schiffbaustrasse 4, 8005 Zurich
Tel. 0041 44 258 77 77
http://www.schauspielhaus.ch/home

Schiffbau was one of the harbingers of the revival of Zurich West. Once known for its factories and warehouses, it is now an increasingly popular entertainment area with numerous bars and restaurants.

A shipyard used to operate here and is credited with the production of two paddle steamers which today are tourist attractions, anchored on the Lake Zurich. Today, Schiffbau is a cultural center which hosts plenty of art events worth your attention. Three stages provide space for theater and dance performances while the huge corridors inside are often taken up by temporary art installations and music concerts.

This post-industrial space, with its high ceilings, enormous windows and vast rooms, is an impressive sight, and provides an unusual backdrop to a range of establishments such as Nietturm, an upstairs bar, or LaSalle, a top-class restaurant offering modern French and Italian inspired cuisine. While it is rather on the pricy side, the daily specials can be a bit cheaper, and you can choose to order a small portion which comes at half the price. Moods, a well known jazz den, is also part of Schiffbau. It offers a packed program of jazz music, with Swiss and international artists performing live every single day of the year.

If you're in a mood for something more casual, head to Les Halles where the eclectic decor includes bikes hung off the ceiling, old posters and random neon signs. Expect buzzing atmosphere and a relaxed attitude to customer service - you have to pay for your drink at the bar and bring it to your table yourself. Mussels are the house specialty but there are plenty of other options available. Before you head out, take a minute to check out the Italian market in the back which offers lots of authentic Italian products.

Schipfe, Old Town

Heimatwerk, Uraniastrasse 1 Zurich, tel. 00 41 44 222 19 55,
http://www.heimatwerk.ch/

Part of the Old Town and definitely on the list of must-see tourist attractions, Schipfe is somewhat less crowded than Bahnhofstrasse or Niederdorfstrasse and can be a more relaxed experience. Walking down the cobbled streets and passing the pretty colorful houses, you'll feel like you have just stepped into a fairy tale.

One of the sites of an early Roman settlement and a medieval fishing district, it later provided an important transfer point for tradesmen sending up their goods along the European rivers. It's seen trades as varied as silk industry and boatbuilding setting up shop here and to this day Schipfe is home to skillful artisans who work and sell their goods here.

Make sure to stop in one of the artisan shops where you can watch craftspeople demonstrate their trade. Leather or iron, antique or just made, it is all there for you to admire - and to buy. If these prove to pricy, head to Heimatwerk, a Swiss handicraft shop run which sells everything from cowbells to jewellery; the only requirement is that it's handmade in Switzerland.

Many of the bars and restaurants in Schipfe operate outdoor gardens in the summer where you can rest for a bit while admiring the river and a line of townhouses on the other bank. It can be quite a romantic spot and a good place for a quiet dinner for two. Check out the Restaurant Schipfe 16 with its charming riverside terrace shaded by a lime tree. You can book a table on a small wooden deck that goes out into the river: unparalleled views of Zurich guaranteed.

From here, take a short walk to Lindenhof, a wonderfully peaceful green space on top of the Lindenhof hill. Once the site of a Roman fort, today it's a tranquil park favored by chess players, and it also offers some amazing views of the whole city.

Zurich Churches

Zurich has three major churches all of which are worth exploring and within easy walking distance of each other.

Grossmünster

Grossmünsterplatz, 8001 Zurich,
tel. 0041 44 252 59 49
http://www.grossmuenster.ch/

The tall towers of Grossmünster, nicknamed "pepper pots" by Richard Wagner, are one of the most recognizable symbols of Zurich. One of them also doubles as a viewing spot - 200 steps will lead you to a breathtaking panorama of the city, with the Alps in the background.

The legend of the three Christian marytrs who were allegedly buried here is as bloody as it is disturbing; it's enough to know that popular belief has it Charlemagne ordered a church to be built on this site after his horse stopped at the martyrs' graves. Construction of the church started in 1100s and lasted over a century.

It was here that Huldrych Zwingli initiated German-Swiss reformation in the early 16th century, an event that transformed Zurich into one of Europe's major centers of religious scholarship. You will see a statue of Zwingli if you walk past the Wasserkirche (Water Church), a small church located on an island on the Limmat, on the way from Grossmünster to Fraumünster.

There is quite a few things inside here worth seeing, from the underground Crypt to the stained glass windows, commissioned in the 20th century. Other modern additions include ornate bronze doors dating from 1935 and 1950. Otherwise, the interiors are rather modest, a result of the Protestant reformation that has stripped the walls and altars of all ornaments.

Outside, it is still quite ornate, with carvings topping the pillars and adorning the portal. A sculpture of seated Charlemagne on the outer wall of the south tower is an interesting sight, as is the more modern statue of Heinrich Bullinger, one of the more prominent Protestant reformers.

Walk into the chapterhouse next to the church and you'll find a 12th century cloister with interesting Romanesque carvings. It provides a much needed quiet space in the middle of the buzzing city.

Fraumünster

Fraumünsterhof 2, 8001 Zurich,
tel. 0041 44 211 41 00
http://www.fraumuenster.ch/

This small church with its slender blue spire has a long history. The Abbey at Fraumünster was established in 853 by Charlemagne's grandson, Louis the German. Many noble women lived here until the Benedictine convent was closed during the 16th century wave of Protestant reforms.

The present church dates from 1250, but the crypt underneath is much older. Just as at Grossmünster, the interior of Fraumünster is far from rich, having lost all its adornments in the 16th century. But Fraumünster has a hidden treasure: a series of stained glass windows designed by Marc Chagall and installed in 1970. Each of these beautifully expressive works of art has a different colour scheme, from orange to blue, rendering the light inside wonderfully intimate.

Walk into the cloister to have a look at the intriguing modern frescoes, designed by Paul Bodmer. The frescoes, which tell the story of how the abbey was founded, bring the story alive with their fresh, dynamic look. Filled with warm light, the cloister is a peaceful place where you can recharge your batteries for the rest of the day.

St. Peterskirche

Schlüsselgasse, 8001 Zurich,
tel. 0041 44 211 50 70
http://www.st-peter-zh.ch/

Although the history of St Peter's Church goes back just as far as that of the other two churches, its present building is much younger.

The church was finished after the Protestant reformation and consequently has always had a modest, almost somber look. Aside from some fresco remains, there isn't really much in the way of sights inside, but it does provide a good space for concerts, held occasionally in the main hall.

Its claim to fame is its clock tower, where you can see the largest clock face in Europe (8.7m in diameter). Try and see how far you can walk away from it before you are unable to read the time anymore. The steeple was used as a "fire watch" since Middle Ages until as late as 1911. The watch looked out for any fires around the city and would fly a flag outside the window each time they spotted one.

Outside the door, you can see the grave of Johan Kaspar Lavater, one of the church's ministers. A friend of Goethe's, he was a popular preacher, so much so that seats had to be reserved in advance for Sunday services. St Peter's is home to a well-known choir, Kantorei St. Peter Zurich, which performs live in the church a few times a year; check the notice board for announcements.

Zurich Museums

Don't forget that museums in Zurich are closed on Mondays.

Zurich Museum of Art

Heimplatz 1, 8001
Zurich, Switzerland
Tel. 0041 44 253 84 84
http://www.kunsthaus.ch/en/

It can take you a good few hours to walk through this impressive museum which is home to a vast collection of Western art, starting from Middle Ages and going all the way to contemporary and even pop-art.

There is some emphasis on Swiss art, giving you a unique opportunity to learn something new about the local culture, but the museum also holds pieces by world famous artists such as J. M. William Turner, Edouard Manet, Henry Matisse, Salvador Dali, Marc Chagall, Vincent van Gogh, Pablo Picasso, and many others, in addition to the largest collection of works by Edward Munch outside of the artist's home country of Norway.

The building itself is also interesting, a modernist 1910 structure designed by the renowned Swiss architect Karl Moser, the first president of the Congres International d'Architecture Moderne.

On a rainy day, walk over to Kulturama, just 10 minutes away. It is essentially a science center with hands-on displays on human body and evolution, and can provide some educational entertainment for kids and adults alike.

Admission is quite pricy with CHF15 per person, but Wednesdays are always free and the museum is open longer. Saturday till Tuesday open from 10am till 6pm (Monday closed), Wednesday - Friday open 10am to 8pm.

Swiss National Museum

Museumstrasse 2, 8021
Zurich, Switzerland
Tel. 044 218 65 11
http://www.nationalmuseum.ch/e/index.php

The 1898 historicist building looks like a castle from long ago, and it does take you on a time journey from prehistory to the 20th century, all within the context of Swiss history. Arts and crafts as well as everyday objects form the bulk of the exhibits, and work well to help you imagine was life was like for our ancestors. The Gothic art section is especially fascinating, as is the armory.

There are interesting sections devoted to the art of clock- and watch-making, although Swiss history is more than just that. You may be surprised to learn about bombs that fell on some Swiss towns during the 2nd World War. Moving on to the 20th century, the museum showcases the finest of Swiss interior design, with displays of sleek modernist furnishings.

Right outside the museum, there's a lovely park which spreads across a tiny peninsula at the confluence of Limmat and the river Sihl. The park is known for its short stint as a legalized drug use area in the late 1980s and early 90s, until its closure in 1992. Since then, it has been a public park and today is a perfect place for a lazy stroll.

There are guided tours in English available but times may vary so call to inquire beforehand. Opening hours are Tuesday till Sunday from 10 am to 5 pm. On Thursdays the museum is open until 7 pm. Admission is CHF10.

Museum of Design

Ausstellungsstrasse, 8005
Zurich, Switzerland
Tel. 0041 043 446 44 67
http://www.museum-gestaltung.ch/en/

This comprehensive museum is devoted to industrial design, architecture and craft and its collections are grouped in four sections: posters, graphics, design and applied art. The curious and fascinating design collection holds examples of packaging from different times and places, from custom-made ornate boxes to factory made cheap plastic cases.

Most of the collections are only available by previous appointment, although frequently updated temporary exhibitions provide a good introduction to the museum's holdings. These exhibitions, each usually only open for a month or two, alternate between Swiss and international themes, and are often created in cooperation with major European design institutes.

Political, cultural and commercial posters from all over the world, including Japan, Cuba, USSR or USA, often form the basis of intriguing temporary exhibitions, organized around a specific theme, such as crime film posters.

The applied art section focuses on everyday objects, from puppets to musical instruments, and is especially famous for its Art Nouveau collection, complete with stunning works by William Morris.

The museum also oversees cultural activities, including art shows, talks, film screenings and concerts.

Open Tuesday-Sunday from 10am to 5pm, except Wednesdays when it closes at 8pm. Admission is CHF9.

Museum Rietberg

Gablerstrasse 15, 8002 Zurich, Switzerland
Tel. 00 41 44 206 31 31
http://www.rietberg.ch/en-gb

Museum Rietberg is a great place to admire great artwork and to relax. Its vast collection of non-European art (Asian, American, African, Oceanian) is spread across several buildings, and displayed in modern ascetic interiors where exhibits are washed in warm, inviting light.

Objects such as masks, figurines and sculptures are often used in imaginative temporary exhibitions which link the past with the present.

If ancient art is your thing, whether you're a fan of Chinese ceramics or pre-Inca finds from Peru, you're in for a treat.

Highlights include an intricate bronze figurine of the Hindu goddess Shiva and a bird-shaped shaman's mask from North America.

Surrounded by a lush garden, the whole museum is a well-planned blend of the old and the new. Historical buildings are complemented by a modern Emerald glass pavilion. The pavilion houses a museum shop with some unique souvenirs on sale, from jewellery modelled after Aztec art to stylish shopping bags and curious key rings.

Enquire about the rich cultural program - although mostly in German, it will probably have an interesting option for a cloudy afternoon, such as a Japanese tea ceremony or a live performance of traditional Indian music.

Open from Tuesday to Sunday, 10am to 5pm, except Wednesdays and Thursdays when it closes at 8pm. Admission is CHF16.

Guild Houses

Zunfthaus zur Meisen

Münsterhof 20, 8001 Zurich,
tel. 0041 44 211 21 44
http://www.zunfthaus-zur-meisen.ch

Haus zum Rüden,

Limmatquai 42, 8001 Zurich,
tel. 41 44 261 95 66
http://www.hauszumrueden.ch/en/lageplan.asp

Zurich has 26 guilds and each of them has its own house, most of them rather impressive in size and style. Each April, the Festival of the Guilds (Sechseläuten) takes place. Guild members participate in a traditional costume parade that culminates in the burning of Böögg, a snowman-shaped cotton doll which symbolizes winter.

Among the Guild houses, Zunfthaus zur Meisen stands out, an imposing baroque building completed in 1757, is home to the Vintners Guild, and also houses a porcelain and faience collection. Notice how the building's two facades are completely different in design, although both equally stunning. Inside, take a look the centuries old paintings on walls and ceilings. The house has been visited by some famous guests in the past, including Winston Churchill and Queen Elizabeth.

Have a look at the Haus zum Rüden as well, originally built in 1348. The ground floor colonnade serves as a walking passage. Inside, admire the Gothic room with its curved wooden ceiling with carved timber heads. You can stay here for a meal - a good-quality, pleasant restaurant operates here now.

Lindt Chocolate Factory

Seestrasse 204, Enge
Tel. +41 (0) 44 716 22 33
http://www.lindt.ch/swf/ger/service/chocolate-shops/lindt-chocolate-shop-kilchberg/

Just south of the city centre, the Lindt Chocolate Factory outlet is a source of great entertainment for all. Not only is the admission free, the chocolate tastings are, too.

Take a tour led by enthusiastic guides who will give you plenty of insider tips on the city itself. After the tour, linger on for a bit: have a cup of hot chocolate or buy sweet souvenirs for the whole family. This is an outlet which means that these world famous treats are much cheaper here than anywhere else.

Open from Wednesday to Friday, 10am to 12pm, and 1pm to 4pm by appointment. Opening times can change without notice so do call ahead of time.

Zurich Zoo & Masoala Rainforest

Zürichbergstrasse 221, 8044 Zürich
Tel. 0041 44 254 25 00
http://www.zoo.ch

The highlight of the Zurich Zoo is definitely the Masoala Rainforest, which has been created with the aim to promote sustainable tourism. Donations are used to fund conservation programs in Masoala National Park in Madagascar. Home to 45 different animal species and over 450 types of exotic plants, including Masoala is not just a place where you can admire the wonders of nature but also an educational center where you will learn about forest conservation.

If you're more into fun than education, make sure to stay for the penguin parade, performed outside each afternoon (weather permitting). The zoo is divided into sections which mirror different geographical areas of the world. The European part is home to water-loving animals such as turtles and storks, while the Himalaya is where you can spot a Siberian tiger or a panda, living in conditions resembling their natural habitats.

For the most scenic route to the zoo, take the number 5 tram from the train station. It will take you up a steep hill and through winding back streets.

Admission is CHF22 but there are discounts for children.

Recommendations for the Budget Traveller

Places To Stay

Design Hotel Plattenhof

Plattenstrasse 26, 07.
Zürichberg, 8032 Zürich
Tel. 0041 44 251 19 10
http://plattenhof.ch

This small boutique hotel, located by a large park, is only a 10-minute walk from Lake Zurich and 15 minutes from Niederdorfstrasse. The facilities are as modern as the design of the spacious rooms, and include a free wi-fi and flat screen TVs with access to XBox. Downstairs, you can grab a bite at the cozy Italian restaurant or the Sento Bar-Lounge. Prices are between CHF195 for single and 250 for double rooms.

The Guests' House

Doeltschihalde 49, 03. Wiedikon, 8055 Zürich
Tel. 0041 44 454 54 54
http://www.theguestshouse.ch/

The decor may seem a little dated but the rooms are kept very clean and have all the modern amenities including free wi-fi and TV with access to VOD. There is also free parking space - partly because the Guests' House is a bit further away from central Zurich.

You can get to Bahnhofstrasse by S-Bahn in about 10 minutes. The trek might be worth it as prices here start at CHF120 and don't go above CHF170, and the staff are helpful and friendly.

Hotel Hottingen

Hottingerstr. 31, 8032 Zürich
Tel. 0041 44 256 19 19
https://www.hotelhottingen.ch/

This hotel is located just 400 meters from the Kunstmuseum and close to all major landmarks, including the lakeside promenade. The design is modern but wooden floors and bright colors add warmth that makes it easy for you to feel at home. Rooms are small but well furnished.

Most rooms are en-suite but some only have access to shared bathrooms so be careful when making a booking. Prices start at around CHF120 for single rooms, with doubles usually around CHF230. There are shared dorms available for women, priced at CHF45 per bed.

Alexander

Niederdorfstrasse 40, 8001 Zürich
Tel. 0041 44 251 82 03
http://www.hotel-alexander.ch

Located in the middle of the Old Town, Alexander Hotel lies within walking distance from Bahnhofstrasse and the river promenade. All the bars and restaurants of Niederdorfstrasse are at your disposal here. Facilities include free wifi and flat screen TVs, and some rooms have mini-bars or refrigerators. The decor is a successful blend of the classic and the modern. Prices for single rooms start at CHF150 and family rooms for three are available at around CHF230.

Hotel Marta

Zähringerstrasse 36, 8001 Zürich
Tel. 0041 44 269 95 95
http://www.hotelmarta.ch/

Newly renovated, Marta hotel lies right outside the Old Town. A 3-minute walk will take you to the Niederdorfstrasse with all its shops, clubs and bars; 5 minutes and you'll be at the main station; and ten minutes is all you need to get to the famous Bahnhofstrasse.

A range of rooms is available, from tiny economy rooms with slanted ceilings (CHF125) to comfortable doubles with large built-in closets and desks priced at CHF225.

Places To Eat & Drink

Lily's Stomach

Langstrasse 197, 8005 Zurich
Tel. 0041 44 440 18 85
http://www.lilys.ch/restaurants

Offering Asian fusion cuisine, this restaurant is always busy but patrons don't seem to mind waiting in long lines until they finally get seated alongside complete strangers at one of the big wooden tables. Open from 11 in the morning till midnight (11am-10.30pm on Sundays), Lily's Stomach offers mains at CHF19 to 23. The extensive menu covers meaty and vegetarian options, and has long sections of wok dishes, soups and grill.

Delicato

Uraniastrasse 40, 8001 Zurich
Tel. 0041 43 344 85 49
http://www.delicato.ch/

This Greek place is most crowded at lunchtime when it offers an all you can eat buffet for CHF25 (weekdays, 11.30am - 2pm).

Stuffed vine leaves, feta salads, moussakas - the list is long and you will certainly not leave this place hungry. Otherwise the prices are Zurich standard with mains around CHF25 each, but you can also get a filling pita bread stuffed with gyros for as little as CHF11.

The place itself is rather small and it might get very busy but if you get a table in the corner then it can be a nice spot for a private dinner.

Open from 11am-2.30 pm and 5.30pm to 12am Monday through Friday; on Saturday, it's only open for lunch from 12am to 2pm. Closed Sundays.

Kaserne-Shilpost

Kasernestrasse 77a, 8004 Zurich
Tel. 0041 44 242 40 00
http://new-points.ch/kaserne

Only 2 minutes from the train station, this large space that can seat 100 guests delivers amazing food inspired by the Turkish and Mediterranean cuisine. Daily menu includes mains that start at CHF17.50, with meaty dishes around CHF20. The menu is diverse, ranging from pasta to fish to lamb dishes.

Open daily from 7am till midnight, except Fridays and Saturdays when it closes at 6pm.

Volkshaus

Stauffacherstrasse 60, 8004 Zürich
Tel. 0041 44 242 11 55
http://www.restaurantvolkshaus.ch/

For some regional Swiss cuisine, go to Volkshaus, established in 1910. With an open-air terrace and a decor that's a blend of modern and traditional (expect chequered tablecloths), it's a great place to try the likes of Fleischkäse mit Pommerysensauce und Bratkartoffeln (meatloaf with pommery sauce and pan-fried potatoes). Swiss cooking is not what you would call vegetarian friendly, so if you're not a meat lover, read the menu before you sit down to makes sure you can find something to your taste.

Mains start at CHF21. Open 8 till midnight, from 10 on sundays with longer hours on the weekend.

Vulkan

Klingenstrasse 33, 8005 Zürich
Telefon 0041 44 273 76 67
http://restaurant-vulkan.ch/contact/

Located right next to the Museum of Design, Vulkan is an Indian restaurant popular with locals, from students to bankers. Fixed price daily specials for under CHF20 are worth attention - there's usually a range of filling curries to choose from. Otherwise mains go up to around CHF30.

Open for lunch from 11am to 2pm daily except Saturdays and Sundays; open for dinner daily from 6pm till midnight.

Places to Shop

Check if you are eligible for tax-free shopping; if your purchases exceed CHF300 and leave the country within 30 days, you may be able to apply for a VAT refund. Go to http://global-blue.com for more details.

Bahnhofstrasse & Niederdorfstrasse

Orell Füssli - The Bookshop
Bahnhofstrasse 70, 8001 Zurich
Tel. 0041 44 211 04 44
http://books.ch

Jamarico
Niederdorfstrasse 51, 8001 Zürich
Tel. 0041 44 261 29 60
http://www.jamarico.ch/home-welcome.html

These two streets are classic shopping destinations although they are mostly associated with pricey designer boutiques. They are worth exploring and there are some hidden gems here. On Bahnhofstrasse, go to Orell Füssli for a great range of books in English. You might be lucky and find the owner reading books to a group of children, something he does on a more or less regular basis. In Niederdorfstrasse, check Jamarico for a good selection of unique T-shirts and some hip fashion at a reasonable price.

16 Tons

Anwandstrasse 25, 8004 Zürich
Tel. 0041 44 242 02 03
http://www.16tons.ch/

Vinyl records, shirts, music related items, and other cool things are what the funky 16tons specialize in. Shopping here is an experience and will appeal to fans of all sorts of music from rockabilly to dancehall. There is a turntable and a headset available for customers to listen to a record before deciding to buy it. Their other location on Engelstrasse sells stylish retro furniture and clothing - a bit more on the pricy side, but still worth taking a look.

Teddy's Souvenir Shop

Limmatquai 34
8002 Zürich
Tel. 0041 44 261 22 89
http://www.teddyssouvenirshop.ch/

From clocks to cowbells, from hats to socks, this is where you can find all your Swiss souvenirs, including but not limited to those related to Zurich. A short walk off Bahnhofstrasse, this is the place to go for some tourist swag, of both the tacky and the classy sort.

Open Monday to Friday 8.30am to 8pm, on Saturdays it closes at 4.30pm. On Sundays Teddy's is open from 10am to 5pm.

Bürkliplatz Flea Market

Flohmarkt am Bürkliplatz - Bürkliplatz, 8001 Zürich
http://www.flohmarktbuerkliplatz.ch/English.html

Located at the lake-end of Bahnhofstrasse and shaded by regal chestnut trees, this is a great place to go shopping on a weekend. You will find as many antiques, second-hand jewellery and other vintage everyday items as you can possibly imagine. Don't miss the flower and vegetable market - it's a nice sight even if you don't want to buy anything, but it closes at 11am.

The market operates from May to October, every Saturday from 6am to 4pm.

Kanzlei Flea Market

Flohmarkt Kanzlei - Kanzleistrasse 56, 8004 Zurich
Tel. 41 79 668 50 40
http://www.flohmarktkanzlei.ch/

This flea market is open all year long. Second-hand items from toys to clothing to furniture are on sale on some 400 stalls. There is a variety of household items on display, including beautiful hand painted mugs which can make an unusual gift. This is shopping in a casual, family-like atmosphere where customers and vendors have known each other for a long time. There is even a supervised play area where children from 3 to 8 can be left with qualified carers. Open Saturdays, 8am to 4pm.

Speciality Market at Zürich Main Station

Spezialitätenmarkt im Hauptbahnhof - Hauptbahnhof, 8001 Zurich

Speciality foods are sold here by vendors from around Switzerland. Meat, cheese,, sweets, drinks, fruit and vegetables, and baked goods will not only make a good snack but also a nice souvenir. Try some Poschiavo bread - a sweet loaf with delicious pear, walnuts and raisins filling, a regional specialty from the south of Switzerland. Open each Wednesday from 10am to 8pm.

Geneva

Located on Lake Geneva with Mont Blanc hovering in the background, Geneva is an idyllic Swiss village at heart. It is the second-largest city in Switzerland and one of the most important world centers of diplomacy, being home to the United Nations (UN) and the Red Cross. Geneva is an exciting, historical, and scenic city to visit.

Geneva is a pleasant and modern city and is a major European financial center. Head down to the lake for an afternoon swim or an evening boat cruise. Take the gondola up the Saleve, and gaze across the beautiful Swiss Alps and down to the Rhone River Valley.

The history of Geneva is typical of so many European cities: power seemed to change hands at the drop of a hat for centuries until the 19th century, when the Napoleonic Wars ended and Geneva entered the Swiss Confederation. About two thousand years ago, Geneva was a fortified town to protect the Roman Empire against Helvetii, a notoriously violent Celtic tribe in the region. The city remained under the auspices of the Holy Roman Empire for another 13 centuries, until the House of Savoy began to rule Geneva, which had been granted a large amount of self-governance.

France had taken much control of the city by the 18th century, however, the French Revolution created another opportunity for Geneva to reclaim its relative autonomy, and after Napoleon left, Geneva joined the Swiss Confederation, leading to centuries of economic stability and prosperity.

Today, Geneva is a fast-paced international financial and political center, with pockets of tiny neighborhoods where you can escape the hustle-and-bustle and enjoy food from anywhere from Afghanistan to Brazil. Head to the lake and go for a morning or afternoon jog, breathing in the crisp Swiss air, and visit impressive Cathedrals, remnants of the strong religious history Geneva has deep down in its roots.

Come to rest your weary feet from an Alpine adventure, stop off on your way to the slopes, and come for the shopping, the food, the culture, and yes, the chocolate. Haven't you heard it's the best in the world?

Culture

Most of the population of Geneva speaks French, however, interestingly; about 40% of the city's population is comprised of foreign nationals. The majority of these people use English or French in offices and in international diplomacy. There are many other languages spoken here and a great number of international eateries where you can get a taste of many other cultures.

Geneva is Switzerland's most international city, and is tucked away at the most western-edge of Switzerland near to the French border. Upon arriving, you will feel that this is a city that takes pride in its buildings, in its streets, and in its reputation.

Geneva is known as the "World's Smallest Metropolis," and many of the larger hotels are located on the right-hand shore of Lake Geneva. On the other side, you have St. Peter's Cathedral and Basilica and the Old Town, which is a charming maze of cobbled roads and small restaurants, as well as a lakeside promenade where you can enjoy an evening stroll in the fresh Swiss air.

Many people visit Geneva for business purposes but come to realize that this city is a stunning cultural attraction in its own right. It's a city to be enjoyed over an extended period of time, sipping a warm cappuccino in the crisp Alpine air, wandering through Old Town or gazing out of a glass window on the 20th story, looking out over the magical fusion of modernity and tradition that is Geneva.

Location & Orientation

Geneva is located in the western-most part of Switzerland and is an extremely accessible city. Its airport is close and convenient to the city, and is also well-served as a hub for the budget airline EasyJet for those of you choosing a thriftier way to fly.

A taxi from the airport into town won't cost very much, but you can also very easily take the number 10 bus, which leaves every 15 minutes from the airport. If you are heading to the train station, get off at stop "22-Cantons." If your destination is the UN Building, then you will want to take bus 5 instead.

Taking the train into Geneva is probably one of the most breathtaking journeys, from any direction, the mountains and heavy forests painting your windows filled with white, blue, and green. The central train station is called CFF, and is centrally-located, serving many destinations in Europe.

Getting around Geneva is very easy with the excellent tram service serving the center of city and the outskirts. You can catch the trams in front of the main train station CFF, and there are stops dispersed around the city, including many in Old Town. Once you're in Old Town, you may want to decide to explore by foot. It can get a bit hilly, but the small alleyways and boutiques are best explored slowly, window-shopping your way through the city.

Climate & When to Visit

Geneva has a fairly mild climate, but can get snow in the city itself in the colder winter months. Expect the summer months to be warm, but still a little chilly at night (that mountain air is pervasive).

July and August can be very busy, with a lot of tourists coming in to share the summer weather in the squares and around the lake, so it may be a good idea to plan your trip for June or September for slightly lower hotel rates and less crowds.

Geneva is a very popular skiing centre in wintertime with many additional flights provided at this time of year. Many ski resorts are on the city's doorstep.

Sightseeing Highlights

Lake Geneva (Boat Cruises & Swimming)

A slow-moving glacier formed Lake Geneva (also known as "Lac Léman). The lake is a crescent-moon shaped body of water that people have flocked to, for pleasure or for pillaging, for millennia. Much of the activity in Geneva, from sports to parks to nightlife, is centered on the shores of the lake. It's not a bad idea to start your visit to Geneva here, then radiate outwards.

Your first stop at the Lake should be the famous "Jet d'Eau", which is an almost 150 meter tall fountain of water, located just off the shore of the center of Geneva. Its central location between the Rhone River and Lake Geneva is purposeful: you can see this fountain from numerous places in the city, and reminds visitors of the importance of the lake to the people living here.

The water jet was built in the late 19th century, and utilizes water from Lake Geneva, which is then pumped through the nozzle at around 500 liters of water per second. For the best view, head to the pier and lighthouse in close proximity to the jet. However; be careful of the wind; sometimes it can change rapidly, and you'll be left knowing what a cool shower of lake water feels like.

Next, venture out beyond the shores and onto the lake itself on a paddleboat steamer cruise. These steamer ships, most of which were commissioned in the early 1900's, offer beautiful vistas, and a sensational panoramic view of Geneva. You can choose a variety of tours, all of which have different ports of call along the river (some of which visit the French side of the river), and even some that will tailor a tour for you.

Daily cruises head to the Lavaux Vineyards or Yvoire, a beautiful medieval town on the shores of the lake. You may even just do a two-hour cruise to gaze at the Alps and stunning natural beauty of the Lake.

For specific tour information, visit the website: http://www.cgn.ch/eng?lan=eng-GB

For a taste of the outdoors, take a bus to Nyon, which is a small town 30 minutes from Geneva International Airport. Nyon is a charming town right on the shore of Lake Geneva. It is located on the road from Geneva to Lausanne, the second-largest city on Lake Geneva, and offers activities in every season.

In the summer, rent a lounge chair on the beach and sunbathe, taking refreshing dips in the lake. In the spring and fall take magnificent hikes through the vineyards, or go biking through the mountains. In the winter, you have endless winter sports opportunities in the Alps, including skiing, snowshoeing and even sleigh adventures.

Nyon Tourism Office
Address: Av. Viollier 8, 1260, Nyon
Telephone +41 (0)22 365 66 00

St. Peter's Cathedral (Old Town)

The city of Geneva is stunning and the lake it is situated upon is gorgeous. You'll want to spend time wandering the cobbled streets of Old Town, nestled right on the shore of the lake. Your exploration of the city should begin here, visiting the historic St. Peter's Basilica.

St. Peter's (St. Pierre) Cathedral belongs to the Swiss Reformed Church, and is the church of Protestant reformer John Calvin. In fact, a chair once used by Calvin remains in the church to this day. The history of the church is much older, however, and extensive excavation has revealed ruins and evidence of a site of worship since the Roman Empire. In the late 700's, the church shared the site with 2 other cathedrals, yet St. Peter's is the only one to remain to this day. When you go inside, make sure you take the time to look at the historic pipe organ and various art works. If you're up for a challenge, climb the towers for a breathtaking view over the city.

Address: Place Bourg-Saint-Pierre 1204 Geneva, Switzerland
Telephone: + 41 (0)22 311 75 75

Upon exiting the cathedral, you'll find yourself in Geneva's Old Town. This area of the city is a wonderful place to get lost in the cobbled alleyways, and spend the afternoon browsing small boutiques or sipping coffee at a sidewalk café. You'll want to head to Maison Tavel, which is a living museum dedicated to Geneva's urban history. Almost the entire house is open to the public, and it serves as a great introduction to life in the city.

Address: Rue du Puits-Saint-Pierre 6 1204 Geneva, Switzerland
Telephone: +41 (0)22 418 37 00

Head to a crossroads just a short walk from the Maison Tavel to where Rousseau was born on the Grand Rue. Gaze down the Rue des Granges, parallel to Grand Rue, at the gorgeous mansions built for Geneva's most affluent residents in the 1700's. You'll want to cross the street towards the Alabama Room, where the Geneva Convention was signed in 1864, and the League of Nations met for the first time sixty years later.

You can explore the interior of the building, most notably the sloped ramp used in the place of stairs. Supposedly this was to accommodate both canons being wheeled up to the ramparts and particularly lethargic councilors who preferred to arrive directly to their meeting room by horseback.

Explore along the Rue du Puits St. Pierre, with its tiny shops and cafes, and to Rue Calvin to see a large collection of non-European art works in the Musée Barbier-Müller at Number 10 Rue Calvin. To get a taste of one of Switzerland's most noted art collections, you should spend a few hours in the Musée d'Art et d'Histoire (The Art and History Museum), on Number 2 Rue Charles Galland. Here you can see work commissioned for St. Peter's Cathedral in the early 15th century on the altarpiece by Konrad Witz, which depicts Jesus and a group of fishermen on Lake Geneva.

Whether you choose to pick a few places of interest and plan your tour of Old Town around them, or you decide to just wander until you happen upon a museum, church, cathedral, or café, at least plan for a long afternoon walking these cobbled streets. You'll want to stay far beyond the sun sets.

United Nations Building

During your visit to Geneva, you have the unique opportunity to visit the second-largest United Nations office (after the United Nations Headquarters in New York City). The United Nations Office in Geneva (UNOG) is located in the stunning "Palais des Nations", built in the 1800's. The Palais is located in the massive Ariana Park, which overlooks the Lake and offers views of Mont Blanc on a clear day. Many member nations contributed to the design of the building, which is said to reflect the stability the UN was aiming for after the widespread destruction of the two World Wars.

While you're here try to see:

- **The Human Rights and Alliance of Civilizations Room**, which is beautifully decorated with art works by Miquel Barceló.
- **The Salle des Pas Perdus**, where you can see a monument that "commemorates the conquest of outer space".
- The place where many significant negotiations have taken place: **The Council Chamber.**

Hundreds of thousands of gifts that have been presented to the Palais and UNOG since its inception.

When planning a tour of the United Nations, keep in mind that this is a working office place, so some corridors or rooms might be closed for meetings. It's best to check the website to make sure on which days the building is open and at which times.

Visitors' Service:
Address: Palais des Nations 14, Avenue de la Paix 1211 Geneva
Tel: +41 (0)22 917 48 96 or +41(0)22 917 45 39

Carouge Neighborhood

Carouge began life in the late 18th century, as a part of the Kingdom of Sardinia. As a result, this tiny suburban area in Geneva has a distinctly Mediterranean feel, from the lively streets to the shade-soaked squares where you can sit and people-watch for hours.

This small annex is separated from Geneva by the River Arve, and seems to be separated by much more. Where Geneva is decidedly Swiss and Alpine, historic and stoic, Carouge is very bohemian, probably not in small part because of the large number of artists and young people living here.

Much of this vibe is earned in part by its history: Carouge was at one time a favorite among Protestants looking to escape at least for an evening the strict laws banning alcohol and dancing in Geneva. Carouge is still busting at the seams with cafes, bars, and nightclubs, and has remained a popular party location for residents and visitors alike. It's an easy river crossing if you use the tram system. It is in fact only a 10-minute ride from the center of Geneva into Carouge.

The first thing you'll notice when entering Carouge is the green shutters on the front of so many of the small three-story houses. The green shutters were part of the original plan of the city when the architects envisioned a city that was a garden in of itself. Inside so many doors and gates, still today, you can see the architects' original vision: each house has a courtyard or a small garden, and the tree-lined streets all lend a garden-feel to this small town. If you want to see a beautiful example of the original architecture, head to Au Vieux Carouge for a taste of delicious Swiss Fondue or more traditional French cuisine. Her you can relax in the cozy interior or the tables sometimes in front of the façade's green shutters when the weather is warm.

Address: Rue Jacques-Dalphin 27, 1227 Carouge, Switzerland
Telephone: +41 (0)22 342 64 98
http://www.auvieuxcarouge.com/

For an unforgettable Swiss Brasserie experience, you should stop by Brasserie la Bourse, which serves traditional brasserie foods such as huge cheese and meat plates and delectable stews made of local rabbit, venison, or beef. This is a cozy venue, tucked away next to a fountain in the center of Carouge, and is very popular with the young residents of the city. Come, grab a table on the sidewalk next to the fountain, and spend hours people-watching the night away.

Address: Place du Marché 7, 1227 Carouge, Switzerland
Telephone: +41 (0)22 300 32 22
http://www.resto.ch/~labourse/index.php/en/

Bastions Park

If you head to the internet, and type in "Geneva, Switzerland" into the search bar, chances are one of the first images that pops up will be the life-sized chess pieces in Bastions Park. Popular with the young, hip Geneva crowd, the Park is filled with activity from the morning until late in the evening, with people jogging, relaxing on the grass or on the benches, or challenging new friends to a game of life-sized chess.

Bastions Park borders Old Town, and there is actually a new wall built right against the old ramparts of the city that delineates the park from the cobbled roads of the Old Town. The rest of the park is lined with trees, some of them remnants of the botanical garden that once stood on this space. The park is a favorite hang-out each day, and one of the best free activities in Geneva. On certain days during the year, however, the park becomes the center of festivities for May Day and a veritable Winter Wonderland around the holidays.

Before your visit, see Geneva's tourism website for special events happening during your visit. Even if you miss the live music and Christmas Trees, however, you'll enjoy your hours spent in Bastions Park, making new friends, or relaxing with old ones. Be sure to brush up on those chess skills.

http://www.geneva.info/parks/

Place du Molarde

No European vacation is complete without a lazy morning spent sipping coffee in a square, people-watching to your heart's content. While in Geneva, you'll want to head into Old Town for the best in people watching, coffee shops, and department stores. Place du Molarde is alive at all hours of the day; during the day, people come to sit, drink coffee, or shop in one of the several department stores or variety of luxury boutique stores.

People also work here, in several of the old office buildings off the square, so don't be surprised if not everyone shares in your sense of laissez-faire during your visit to the square. Avoid the bustling suits, and have a seat, and enjoy the sun as you read a book and enjoy a glass of wine or beer, coffee, or hot chocolate.

The most visible sight in the square is the national monument, built in the late 18th century, that is placed in a huge fountain in the center of the square. Also not to miss is the military tower dominating one of the corners of the square, which in the 1300's was a blockade that protected the port of Molarde.

For an unforgettable café experience, head to number 5 in the Place du Molarde, to the Café du Centre, which is one of the several cafes with outdoor terraces year-round. Not to worry: in the frosty winter months, the tables are usually ensconced in a thick clear plastic tent, and you'll be heated by gas lanterns while cozying up inside. The café also offers food, and is a great place to people-watch, relax, or enjoy a hearty stew or light snack during a break in your touring.

Paquis (Beach, Baths & Ethnic Eateries)

Paquis is a glorious juxtaposition of wealth and charm. On one side of the coin, this is one of the most affluent districts in Geneva, and is located in the center of the city, between the main railway station and Lake Geneva.

Here is where the rich and famous come to live and play, and if your budget is less rigid, you can stay amongst them, in the Beau-Rivage, Hilton, or Bristol, some of the most expensive hotels in the city.

The good news here is that while many of the places to stay are quite expensive, tucked amongst the wealth and carved marble are some inexpensive and free activities, including swimming in the lake from the gorgeous beach at Des Bains des Paquis. You may need to put a little money down to rent a lounge or umbrella, but setting your towel down on the sand is free, and you'll have a spectacular view of the huge fountain in Lake Geneva, the white lighthouse, and the windsurfers and water-skiers all carving their way through the crystal clear waters. The baths on the site are also open year-round, and you'll find several cafes and restaurants to satiate you after an afternoon in the sun, or a Swedish massage at the baths.

Now, the secret to this neighborhood, again, is to duck behind these high-end attractions, and explore the eight square blocks (Rue des Alpes/Rue de Lausanne/Lake Geneva/Parc Mon'Repos) that are filled with restaurants representing cuisine from dozens of countries. Also, you'll want to come here for an incredible (and affordable) shopping experience: make a first stop at Rue des Paquis to scope out the new and used books in the small book traders, make an investment in some locally-crafted silver jewelry, or even buy an authentic oriental rug.

When you're finished shopping, take your pick of the dozens of restaurants in Les Paquis, some Japanese, some Chinese, some Moroccan, to taste authentic ethnic cuisine. It's a good idea to bring along enough cash, as many of the restaurants in this neighborhood still do not accept credit cards.

Your night doesn't end when the check arrives, however. After dinner, head to an authentic Middle Eastern lounge where you can smoke shisha (flavored tobacco) while sipping on wine or tea on huge comfy cushions. The hours will slip away, in a mellow smoky haze, while you relax, chat with the people on neighboring cushions, or tucked away in a corner sharing a romantic evening out.

Plainpalais Flea Market

We all enjoy a good bargain. For an incredible locally-flavored experience, head to the Plainpalais Flea Market, and put on your bargaining hat. You'll need those skills here. Located in the huge open space at 1204 Plainpalais, this space was once used for quarantine for people sick with a contagious illness, but is now used, not only for the famous flea market, but also several times a year for when the circus comes to town, or during Christmas time, when European Christmas Markets pop up in every corner of Geneva.

The flea market is open every Wednesday and Saturday, rain or shine. You can find just about anything you didn't know you wanted here, including a DVD of You Got Mail, or a CD of your favorite Aerosmith album. If you're in the market for some antiques or super-hip 70's or 80's used furniture, this is the place to be, and if you're planning on staying in Geneva for a while, may be a great and cheap way to decorate and furnish your new digs.

Whether you're looking for a bierstein to bring home, or an antique shoe horn, the Plainpalais Flea Market is a perfect place to bargain and browse the day away.

Museum of the Red Cross

Now in the midst of a major expansion project that will greatly expand the museum's exhibit and public spaces, the Museum of the Red Cross is planning a huge re-opening in early 2013. Head to the website to learn more about the expansion, and when the museum will be re-opened.

Even though the new museum will be organized differently than the former lay-out, you can expect a comprehensive photography collection that follows Red Cross and Red Crescent activity in hundreds of disasters around the world. It is a stunning display of humanitarian effort, and a very moving display. follows Red Cross and Red Crescent activity in hundreds of disasters around the world. It is a stunning display of humanitarian effort, and a very moving display.

You can also expect to learn about the founder Henry Dunant, and the history of the importance of Red Cross during the World Wars. An exciting addition to the exhibits will the Geneva Convention, originally written in 1864, and an excellent visual display focused on the importance of the Convention and of Conventions ratified in 1949 that aim to protect innocent civilians during times of conflict.

The museum is very accessible by public transport, and when re-opened will offer a worthy use of a morning or an afternoon marveling at the prolific good deeds done by the Red Cross and Red Crescent since its inception.

http://www.micr.ch/index_e.html

The Saleve (Swiss Alps)

Well, it would be almost a sin to visit Geneva and not at least dip your feet a little in the beauty of the Swiss Alps, rising up around the city. An excellent day-trip from Geneva is The Saleve, easily accessible by public transportation, and such a beautiful Swiss landscape, you may find yourself singing the lines to The Sound of Music's The Hills are Alive! (although that was actually filmed in Salzburg, Austria).

One of the things you should experience is the cable car ride to the top of The Salve, for a sensational view of Mont Blanc and the Swiss Alps. The panoramic views of the mountains will absolutely take your breath away, and even if your trip to The Saleve is limited only to this cable car ride, you'll feel you've had at least a taste of the Alps.

Head to this website for times and days of opening. During extremely windy times, the cable car may not be open, so it's good to check before you go.

http://www.telepheriquedusaleve.com/

In addition to travelling up the cable car and marveling at the views, you might also want to try your hand at parasailing, hiking, or mountain biking, all of which are possible in this area of the Alps. Many of these adventures are family-friendly, so if you have children along, or if flinging yourself off a cliff strapped to a set of nylon wings isn't your cup of tea, you can choose an easier hike, or mountain biking along more level paths. For a great starting point of your trip, head to the Mountain's website to explore all the adventurous possibilities for your trip:

http://www.myswitzerland.com/en/mount-saleve.html

To get to The Saleve, take bus 8, 34, or 41 from the center of Geneva to Veyrier-Ecole. If you are driving, just head straight to Veyrier, right on the French border, to park underneath the cable car.

Recommendations for the Budget Traveller

Places to Stay

While some neighborhoods in Geneva are understandably quite expensive to stay in, you'll be surprised at the hidden gems you'll find to give you a stay you'll never forget. Here are a few.

Hotel Central

This centrally located hotel (about 10 minutes from Old Town) is a great bargain, and a fine place to hang your hat for your visit.

Breakfast can be delivered to your room between 7 am and 9 am. Rooms have a mini-fridge so you can tuck away some chocolates for dessert in bed. The service is warm and personal, and rooms clean and comfortable.

Address: 2, rue de la Rotisserie, Geneva CH-1204, Switzerland
Telephone: +41 (0) 022 818 81 00
http://www.hotelcentral.ch/
Price range: USD 100 – 200

Appart'Hôtel Résidence Dizerens

While the name is a mouthful, the hotel itself is very budget-friendly, and centrally located in Geneva. The guesthouse is actually located on a pedestrian street in the city, tucked away from the traffic of the main streets. Each tiny apartment has its own kitchenette, which makes saving money on meals as easy as pie. Each room has a TV and DVD player, if you simply must spend an evening in. A bonus is the laundry facility located on premises, as well as its location, only about a 10-minute walk from the University of Geneva.

Address: Rue Dizerens 7 Geneva CH-1204, Switzerland
Telephone: +41 (0)22 809 61 11
http://www.apparthotel-residence-dizerens.rooms-easy.com/
Price range: USD 100 – 140

Ibis Geneve Central Gare Hotel

This clean and efficient hotel is perfect for travelling business people interested in fast internet and a central location, as well as tourists more into the polished feel of a chain hotel than a guesthouse. It is located in the city center, right near the Grand Casio, and features a bar in the premises that is open 24/7: perfect for that night-cap before bed after a long day's touring.

Address: Rue Voltaire 10 Geneva CH-1204, Switzerland
Telephone: +41 (0)22 338 20 20
http://www.accorhotels.com/gb/hotel-2154-ibis-geneve-centre-gare/index.shtml

Places to Eat & Drink

Buvette Bains des Paquis

Located in the diverse and charming Paquis neighborhood, this probably is one of the most interesting dining experiences you can have in Switzerland. The Buvette is set in the Bains des Paquis, and is a perfect cherry on top of a day lounging on the beach or in the baths. The restaurant has a small terrace that is open when the weather allows it, and offers superb views of the Jet d'Eau (fountain), water-sports on the Lake, and the Kempinski Hotel.

The "interesting" aspect comes when the clients of the Turkish baths on the premises emerge from the baths naked to head to the decks to warm up in the sun. If this doesn't faze you, you simply must not miss the famous "Champagne Fondue" served from September through April. Reservations are a must for these months, but recommended year-round. No credit cards are accepted here, so be sure to check out the menu online and bring the appropriate amount of cash.

Address: 30 quai du Mont-Blanc, Les Pâquis, Geneva, 1201
Telephone: +41 (0) 227381616
www.buvettedesbains.ch

Le Thé

A day bargaining at the Plainpalais Flea Market is bound to whet your appetite! For a deliciously authentic Asian culinary experience, head to Le Thé, and try the dim sum, tapioca, and delicate shrimp crepes. Even if you're only in the mood for a pot of tea, this restaurant is worth a peek, but if you plan on staying for a meal, then it's advisable to call ahead for a reservation. Once you're finished eating, you may want to walk to 5 Rue des Savoises for the restaurant's own shopping emporium Dragon Art, in case you want to shop for Asian-themed souvenirs or a box of tea to bring home with you. Bring cash, as no credit cards are accepted here.

Address: 65 rue des Bains, Plainpalais, Geneva, 1205
Telephone: +41 079 4367718

Chez Ma Cousine

Your travels will without a doubt bring you into Old Town, and a scrumptious dinner can be found at this charmingly decorated restaurant. However, there is something special about this particular restaurant: they do only three things, and they do them perfectly. For lunch or dinner, you can expect the following: a roast chicken (whole if you are a couple, a half if you are ordering single portions), potatoes, and a crisp salad. That's it. No muss, no fuss. The chicken is roasted to perfection, and at less than 15 Swiss Francs per person, this is certainly a meal you can sink your teeth into. Plus, the people watching here is unparalleled.

Address: 6 place du Bourg-de-Four, Vieille Ville, Geneva, 1204
Telephone: +41 (0)22 3109696
Website: www.chezmacousine.ch

Maison Rouge

You absolutely won't want to miss this unique dining experience, located just North of Carouge, across the river from Geneva. The name means "Red House," and the restaurant is just that: a big, red house. What makes this place so special is that the owner cooks all the dishes himself. Miraculously, while feeding his guests, he will find time to wander out of the kitchen, chat with the guests and make sure everyone's having a good time. A real gem, and a dinner you won't soon forget.

Rue des Noirettes 17, Geneva 1227, Switzerland
+4122 342 00 42
http://www.lamaisonrouge.ch/

Places to Shop

Geneva is a shopper's dream: from huge department stores, to specialty chocolate or clothing boutiques, to the flea markets and seasonal Christmas Markets, there's sure to be something for just about anyone, including the friends and family back home. In Switzerland, expect most stores to be closed on Sundays, and also closed (with the exception of the larger department stores) from 2:00 – 4:00 pm on weekdays. Here are some shopping locations not to miss:

If you are in the market for a Swiss watch, you've come to the right place: the watch industry in Switzerland dates to the 17th century and Geneva is the place to find the perfect one. Head to either **Expace Temps or Bucherer**, located on Rue du Mont Blanc 13and 22, respectively. Even if a new watch is not in your budget for this trip, you can still head to the **Piaget** store at Rue du Rhone 40 for a window-shopping experience you won't soon forget.

A slightly more affordable gift for yourself or loved ones is some prized Swiss chocolate. Of course, you are in Switzerland so really you could stop of at the grocery store or local market for some of the best chocolate you've ever tasted, but here are some other options for a more artisanal chocolate experience.

The Cartier Patisserie Confiserie Chocolaterie, on Route de Suisse 38, is your golden ticket to the best sweets and pastries you could imagine. For over 150 years, the Cartier family has sold chocolates to the residents and visitors of Geneva, and remains a favorite. Plan on sitting down or a few minutes and pairing that chocolate croissant or truffle with a cappuccino or if you're brave, even a cup of molten hot real chocolate, topped with a dollop of whipped cream. Decadence at its best, and one of the city's shining jewels.

http://www.cartier-swiss.ch/

Also a historical chocolate store, **Rohr** is another family-run business that will have your heart fluttering and your mouth watering for more. Head to the Place du Molard, and you'll find Rohr tucked into number 3, offering an excellent respite from a long day's touring.

http://www.rohr.ch/en/

Geneva is a window-shopper's paradise. If you're more into the gazing than the buying, you want to be sure to head to these neighborhoods. Not only do they offer the best shopping opportunities in the city, but it's in these neighborhoods that you'll discover that alongside hiking and skiing, window-shopping is practically a sport in Switzerland. The people watching is sensational, and the restaurants and cafes here are perfect oases when you've reached your shopping (or credit card) limit.

Rue du Mont Blanc: This street, and several streets surrounding it, offer a wide variety of clothing shops and jewelry stores, and is a perfect place to pick up mementos of your vacation, or gifts of Swiss Pocket Knives for your friends back home.

Old Town: You must get lost here to truly appreciate how magical this part of Geneva is. Each twist and turn reveals a small store, a boutique, an artisan's studio and store. What is an extra-special treat is finding one of the dozens of small antique stores, which really should be called museums, as artifacts and art works from the Middle Ages can be bought (at a price) here. Ask the shop owner the history of the piece, and you'll be surprised how excited some owners are to tell you about how they acquired the piece, and what its historical significance is.

Manor Department Store, on Rue Cornavin 6 (+41 (0) 22 909 4699), is one of the largest department stores in Geneva, and is known throughout the country for its variety of clothing collections, electronics, and perfumes. An added treat is the food market, located on the ground floor, which is popular with locals taking a break during the workday.

http://www.manor.ch/

Printed in Great Britain
by Amazon